THE WHEEL OF THE ARTS IN ACADEMICS

BY

ELEANOR RUSSELL-BROWN

Sarasota, Florida

Copyright © Eleanor Russell-Brown, 2018

All rights reserved. Published by the Peppertree Press, LLC.
The Peppertree Press and associated logos are trademarks of
the Peppertree Press, LLC.

No part of this publication may be reproduced, stored in a retrieval
system, transmitted in any form or by any means, electronic,
mechanical, photocopying, recording, or otherwise, without prior written
permission of the publisher and author/illustrator.
Graphic design by Rebecca Barbier.

For information regarding permission,
call 941-922-2662 or contact us at our website:
www.peppertreepublishing.com or write to:
the Peppertree Press, LLC.
Attention: Publisher
1269 First Street, Suite 7
Sarasota, Florida 34236

ISBN: 978-1-61493-562-9

Library of Congress Number: 2018900970

Printed April 2018

I have designed a program entitled,
'THE WHEEL OF THE ARTS IN ACADEMICS"
for students grades five to twelve.
The program integrates music, art, poetry, drama, and dance
into any one of the academic subjects.

There are fifteen stories with activities in the book.

- First, I write a short story.

Next is a series of activities that correlate with the story such as:

- Composing music
- Writing poetry
- Creating a dance, such as the Scottish
- Creating plays, skits, humorous writings
- Guest speakers and musicians

Some students like to present art, perhaps with music background provided by another student. Several students can work together on one project in this program. Students need to have access to a computer or dictionary for finding any terms or words for use in their presentations.

The teacher is merely the facilitator in this program—the student is the creator. What with the arts being taken out of curriculum, this program fills the vacancy for the student who requires the need for developing his/her artistic nature. It can be done successfully by using the arts and academics concurrently.

Eleanor Russell-Brown

INDEX

1   AEGAR'S DIGGER DANCE........................4
Activities
Aegar's Digger Music & Melody

2   TOADY'S JIG...12
Activities
Toady's Jig Music & Melody

3   GERTIE..22
Activities
Gertie Jig Music & Melody

4   THE HOME COMFORT............................26
Activities
The Home Comfort Waltz & Melody

5   GANDLY...30
Activities
Gandly Music & Melody

6   SATURDAY NITE...34
Activities
Saturday Nite Music & Melody

7   JOE PYE..36
Activities
Joe Pye Music & Melody

8 THE COW PASTURE 40
Activities
The Cow Pasture Music & Melody

9 CASSIE 44
Activities
Cassie Music & Melody

10 DREAMS THAT I DREAMED 48
Activities
Dreams That I Dreamed Music & Melody

11 THE DD TREE.......................................54
Activities
The DD Tree Music & Melody

12 THE SUGAR SLED..................................60
Activities
The Sugar Tree Sled Music & Melody

13 KITTENS IN THE HAYSTACK 66
Activities
Kittens in the Haystack Music & Melody

14 FIDDLE IN THE ATTIC...........................70
Activities
Fiddle in the Attic Music & Melody

15 PHOEBE 74
Activities
Phoebe Music & Melody

1

AEGAR'S DIGGER DANCE

When we moved into an old farmhouse, we noticed an overgrown graveyard across the highway.

A beautiful iron fence with a fancy gate, like the kind you would see at the entrance to a very big mansion, surrounded one group of gravestones. One stone inside the fence was much taller than the rest and very ornate.

We were curious about the cemetery, so one day my sister and I trampled through the tall grass and berry bushes to get to the gate. It wasn't easy to open because it was so old and rusty.

We saw a tall stone that was engraved with a name. It read: Joshua Aegar. Below his name were more scratched words. He was a Revolutionary War soldier and the epitaph on his stone read:

JOSHUA AEGAR
A GALLANT SOLDIER AND HERO.

Below that were his dates of birth and death. They were very blurred. We could only see 178 something. The rest had been wiped out with age.

I wonder what he did that made him a hero.

Our neighbor told us that he had seen the ghost of Mr. Aegar come out sometimes at night and dance around his grave. I really wanted to see that and I told the neighbor to come over to get me when saw the ghost again.

But he never did—I think he was trying to scare me, but I wasn't scared, just curious.

Activity #1 (Art, Music)
Make a puppet of Aegar

Materials:
- Scissors
- Black cloth for body
- Pipe cleaners
- Needle and thread
- Quilt stuffing or any scrap material
- Felt or cardboard for the hat
- String
- Doweling
- Small pieces of cardboard for the shoes
- Crayons
- Paint
- Markers
- String or embroidery floss for the hair
- Paste or glue

1. Cut a circle out of the black cloth using a cardboard circle as a template.
2. For lower grades - pull the top together and staple, leaving a small hole to put stuffing in. For upper grades, pull the top together and sew loosely, leaving part of the thread hanging so you can pull it together. When through, it should look like a fat stomach.
3. Draw a smaller circle for the head. Use instructions above.
4. Glue the head to the body.
5. Glue or sew the pipe cleaners to the body for arms. Bend them any way you want to.
6. Glue or sew pipe cleaners to the bottom of the stomach for legs and bend them in a dancing form.
7. Glue string to the head for the hair.
8. Using your marker, draw eyes, nose and a mouth, or use buttons or thread.
9. Glue the string to his chin and sides of his cheeks for a beard.
10. Research the shape and kind of hat for that time in history, then measure for the size you want.
11. To move arms and legs, tie strings to the wrists and legs. Then tie the string to the doweling.

Activity #2 (English, Drama, Music, Art)
Make a Puppet Theater

Materials:
- Cardboard boxes
- Markers
- Paints
- Cloth
- Tape
- Staples
- String, Needle and Thread (for upper grades)

1. Find a cardboard box that is longer rather than wide.
2. Cut a hole in the front and back, or cut a hole only in the top if you prefer to work your puppet from that angle. (Leave the front open).
3. Paint or color the box.
4. Cut enough cloth to fit from the top of the box to the bottom.
5. Staple or sew a hem wide enough for doweling to go through.
6. Slip the doweling through the hem of the cloth.
7. Cut a round hole a little bigger than the doweling in both ends of the box and slip the doweling through. Secure the doweling with masking tape. Make sure you leave enough cloth so that it comes together when you close the curtain.
8. Set the box on a desk or table.

For props, make a tombstone and a fence out of cardboard, or draw long grass on the inside back of the box with a tombstone and a fence.

Activity #3 (English, Drama, Music, Art)
Put on a Puppet Show

This activity is for the classes in activity one and two.

Put on a puppet show following the story line.

Materials:
- Pencil and paper
- A keyboard with different sound effects
- The puppets & the puppet theater

Activity #4 (Music, Math, English)
Compose a Song about Mr. Aegar

Since most students don't know how to write a song,
you will have to teach them how. Or — allow the student who chooses
this activity to make up his/her own song by ear on the keyboard.

Materials:
Lined music paper (copy the staff sheet I have provided at the end of the book)
Keyboard

1. Draw the music staff on the board.
2. Put 5 notes on the staff — ranging from G above middle C, to D2.
3. Instruct them to only use those notes. Put the notes on the staff.
4. Limit the time signature to 4/4.
5. Put a quarter note, an eighth note, a half note and a whole note on the board. Beside each one, show how many counts it gets.
6. Tell them that each measure has to add up to 4 counts, or beats. Demonstrate.
7. Show them how to rhyme words, then fill in the rest of the words — ghost, roast, toast, most, boast, coast, host, post.
8. If you choose ghost and boast, you might make this sentence; Mr. Aegar was a ghost, he was a hero he did boast.
9. Make 2 more sentences and that is the entire song.
10. Show how to put the words under the notes. Demonstrate how sometimes one word can go under 2 notes.
11. When finished, play and sing each song for them. It was my experience that they eagerly lined up to hear their song performed on the piano by me. Some can sing and perform their own song.

Some of the older students who study an instrument will want to use sharps and flats, with various time signatures. Let them. Creativeness is what's important in song writing. Student can also use the melody in their fiddling tune for "AEGAR'S DIGGER DANCE".
(The melody is at the end of the activity).

Suggestions for song titles:

"Stepping Out Of Time"   "Stepping Into The Future"   "Aegar Steps Out"
Record their songs

Activity #5 (Music, Math, English)
Write a Poem

Write a poem or a commercial about "Aegar's Digger Dance. - Try some Haiku poetry.
Suggestions for titles:

The Night Dance

Come Dance With Me I'm a Hero

Illustrate with art or music background for your background

Each student will read his/her poem to the class

Print out the poems for the students

Activity #6 (English, Physical Education, Drama, History)
Act out a commercial about Aegar's Digger Dance

Write and act out a commercial about "Aegar's Digger Dance".

Put these vocabulary words on the board for learning and using in the commercial:

epitaph, revolution, enemy, historian.

Suggestions for commercial topics:

- "Digger's Dance Studio, Learn to dance like a ghost in one lesson —You'll never forget how again! Call 000-DOWNUNDER"
- "So you want to be a soldier! Join the Revolutionary War! Get a medal for bravery! Sign up in the dark room down at the general store!"
- "EPITAPHS FOR SALE — SOMETHING SPECIAL EVERYONE SHOULD HAVE! Email is lastwordsisay.jump YOU WON'T BE SORRY — EVERYONE WILL LOVE WHAT THEY READ ON YOUR GRAVESTONE!"
- GHOST CATCHERS, Ltd. - Use props and costumes
- Limit each commercial from one to three minutes

Activity #7 (Music, Drama, Physical Education)
Create a dance to "Aegar's Digger Dance"

This activity is fun for Music, Drama, Physical Education classes

Create a dance to "Aegar's Digger Dance".

Use the jig for the dance.

Students who are taking dancing lessons could use one of their dance steps for the presentations.

Use props and costumes such as scarves.

Activity #8 (History, English, Drama, Art)
Write a Play or Skit about Mr. Aegar

Research some facts about the Revolutionary War, such as cause, length, outcome, and countries involved. Suggestions for titles:
- *Stepping Out*
- *Nighttime at Aegar's Grave Site*
- *Joshua Aegar, The Hero*
- *Hat on Backwards, Marches Wrong Way*

Use props, art, and costumes for the presentations.

Activity #9 (Music, Art, History)
Draw a Scene from "Aegar's Digger Dance"

Suggestions:
Mr. Aegar dancing. Mr. Aegar dressed as a Revolutionary War Hero. The graveyard. An epitaph on his gravestone. Show and tell for the presentations.

Activity #10 (History)
Guest Speaker, Historian

Invite a historian to the class who can tell some anecdotal facts about the Revolutionary War and about old cemeteries in the area. Before the speaker comes in, ask the students to write some questions for a Q & A session after the lecture.

Suggestions:
- Why did Mr. Aegar have a fancy fence around his tombstone?
- Why did they have to wear such a funny looking hat in that war?
- Why was he a hero?

Activity #11 (Psychology)
Guest Speaker

Invite a paranormal psychologist to the class who can discuss whether or not ghosts exist.

Activity #12 (History)
Field Trip to Old Cemetery

Go on a field trip to an old cemetery and do gravestone rubbings.

Activity #13 (Music)
Guest Musician

Invite a fiddler in to play some fiddling tunes, including "AEGAR'S DIGGER DANCE."

AEGAR'S DIGGER DANCE

Allegro

Eleanor Russell Brown

2

TOADY'S JIG

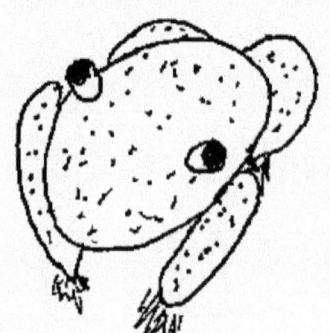

After a rain or a storm, I liked to go out and look for frogs and toads. Then I put them in a bucket with some grass and stones.

Sometimes I raced them to see if the great big frogs out-hopped the little tiny ones. I decided that the little ones hopped faster than the big ones, but the big ones could hop higher and farther, so the big toads usually won.

One day my father came over to where I was sitting on the lawn. He wondered what I was so interested in as I looked down in my bucket.

He looked down into the bucket and saw all those frogs and toads.

"Mmm," he said, "Did you pick up those toads?"

"Yeah," I answered.

"Well," he went on, "Did you know that you can get warts all over your hands from touching toads?"

I looked up at him and then looked down at my hands, turning them over and over. I danced all over the lawn, shaking my hands so that any warts would fall off. I didn't have any though.

I found out later that the toad-wart-thing is an old wives tale.

Activity #1 (Art)
Make a Frog or Toad Puppet

Materials for lower grades:
- Green or gray sock
- Glass beads or buttons for eyes black marker for the warts glue
- Cotton stuffing

For upper grades (5-8)
- Paper mache
- Fabric
- Thread and needle
- Glue and newspaper

Follow the instructions in "Aegar's Digger Dance" for making the puppet (see page 5)

Activity #2 (Art)
Make a Puppet Theater

Follow the directions in activity #2 for "Aegar's Digger Dance". (see page 6)

Activity #3 (Drama, Music)
Put on a Puppet Show

Refer to Aegar for instructions. (see page 8)

Activity #4 (Music)
Compose a Song about Toady

Follow the directions in Activity #4 to "Aegar's Digger Dance", for writing a song.

Suggestions for titles: *Warts Be gone! Toad, Frogs & Races.*

Perform the song for the presentations.

Activity #5 (English, Drama, Art)
Write a poem about Toady

Rhyme words like: *Warts, Hand, Dad, Race, Frog, Toad.* Try some Haiku.

Suggestions for titles:

Toady, Frogs, Hand in Hand, Old Wives Tale.
- Illustrate with art
- Students read poems in class

Activity #6 (Science, Music, Art)
Draw the Scene

Suggestions:

- The girl/boy looking at their hands
- The father standing at the scene looking down
- The toad/frog race.
- A bucket full of jumping toads and frogs
- A beautiful colorful toad or frog. (tell why it's colorful)

Show and tell about the art at the presentation.

Activity #7 (English, Physical Education, Drama, History)
Write and Act out a Commercial for Toady's Jig

Write and act out a commercial for Toady's Jig.

Put the following vocabulary words on the board for learning and using in the commercial: *endangered, species, genus, warts, cure, amphibian.*

Suggestions:

The great toad/frog race will be held at the Grange Hall. Sign up to enter your toads or frogs. First prize will be a Brazilian tree frog! (instructions for care included)

The race is for the benefit of "THE ERADICATION OF WARTS FOUNDATION". Don't be bashful—hop right in!

WARTS BE GONE! Dr. Jones treatment will make your warts disappear overnight! Send a check or money order today. (no CODs)

> TO: Dr. Jones Disappearing Act,
> NOWHERE TO BE SEEN, USA, 000000.

BREAKING NEWS ON A CURE FOR WARTS!
STAY TUNED FOR FURTHER UPDATES!

Use props, art, and costumes for presentations.

Activity #8 (Science)
Guest Speaker-Environmentalist

Invite an environmentalist to the classroom to talk about the disappearance of frogs.

Ask questions such as:
- Do peepers that we hear in the springtime turn into frogs?
- How do old wives tales get started?
- How long can a frog stay underwater?
- How long does a frog or toad live?
- Why do toads have warts and frogs don't?

Activity #9 (Physical Education, Music)
Create a Dance to Toady's Jig

Use the jig music for the dance.

Use props and costumes for the presentations.

Activity #10 (English, Drama)
Write and Act out a Play or Skit about Toady's Jig

Suggestions for titles: *Look, but don't touch! The old wives tale.*

Use props, costumes and background music for the presentations.

Activity #11 (Science)
Guest Speaker-Medical Professional

Invite a medical student or a dermatologist in to talk about warts and their cause.

Activity #12 (Science)
Guest Speaker-High School Student

Invite a high school student in to explain the physics of the higher hops vs. the longer hops.

Activity #13 (Music)
Guest Musician

Invite a fiddler in to play some Toady fiddling tunes.

3

Gertie

Gertie was a goat. He did all sorts of weird things, like attempting to eat tin cans. I liked to go out by his tree where he was sometimes tied up and pet him.

About now I can imagine that you are wondering how a he-goat could have a she-goat name. Well, I didn't know which he was when he was little, so I just named him whatever came to mind.

After a few visits though, I learned that he wasn't so nice.

One day when I turned to walk away from him, he chased me and bunted me right on my back side.

Maybe he didn't like his name.

Activity #1 (Music)
Compose a Song about Gertie

Follow the directions in "Aegar's Digger Dance" for composing a song. Students can make up their own melody, or use the one for "Gertie".

Suggestions for titles:

A She-Goat Got To Be a He-Goat, Gertie Didn't Like His Name, or *Gertie, You Got My Goat*

Activity #2 (English)
Make up a Poem about Gertie

Suggestions for titles:

Gertie, Gertie, Why Are You So Mean? Tin Cans Are So Yummy, Don't Like Gertie Any More
Illustrate the poem with art. Print out poems.

Activity #3 (Art, Drama)
Write and Act Out a Commercial for Gertie

Use props and art. Suggestions: Has Someone got 'cher goat? Call, 'GIT BACK Inc., for the solution to yer problem. GOATS GALORE, INC. The number one company that will fix you up with a non-bunting goat. 30 day guarantee on all goats while they last.
How to tame a goat in only 24 hours. CALL 'NANNY NICE' ANY TIME AT: 000-000-111

Activity #4 (Physical Education)
Create a Dance for Gertie

Use the "Gertie Jig" for the music.

Activity #5 (Music, Art)
Draw the Scene

Suggestions:
Gertie eating a can. Gertie chasing the girl. Gertie with a goatee.
Show and tell about the drawing using the "Gertie Jig" as background music.

Activity #6 (English, Drama)
Write a Play about Gertie

Use any interpretation of the topic, "Got 'Cher Goat!"
Suggestions for titles:

What's in a Name? Gertie Got My Goat! So You Don't Like Your Name!
How Would You Like To Go To The Meat Factory, 'Friend'?

Would you be friends with Gertie again after what she did? Write and tell why.

Activity # 7 (Science)
Guest Speaker, Goat Farmer

Invite a farmer in to talk about goats.

Ask questions about:

    What kinds of goats do they have?

    Are the goats really mean?

    Why do people have goats on their farm?

Activity #8 (Music)
Guest Musician

Invite a fiddler in to play the jig for Gertie, (in the back of this story) plus any other jig.

GERTIE (MELODY)

ERB

4

THE HOME COMFORT

THE HOME COMFORT was an old wood stove that my mother used to cook on and bake in. But I liked it for other things too.

On a cold winter night, I crawled around in back of the stove on the warm floor while I read comic books. As I sat there reading, I could smell the bread baking and I couldn't wait to have some with lots of homemade butter on my slice.

My sister and I also had fun with our dog Tricksy and her puppies. We had made a cozy bed for her and her little family in the wood box, then we dressed them all up.

Tricksy was such a nice little dog. She just laid there and patiently waited until we were through playing with her puppies, then she and her little family fell asleep by the stove.

Dogs like to feel warm and cozy, too.

Activity #1 (Music, English)
Compose a Song about The Home Comfort

Follow the directions in Aegar's Digger Dance, activity #4.

Suggested titles:
> *Crawlin'Round in Back, MMM, I Smell Bread', My Dog Tricksy*

Use THE HOME COMFORT melody for the words.

Activity #2 (English)
Write a Poem about Home Comfort

Some words for the poem: *stove, bake, bread, book, crawl, dog, warm, puppies.*

Activity #3 (Physical Education, Art, Drama)
Write and Act Out a Commercial for Home Comfort

Suggestions:
> Old style cookin' lessons for only $3.00 BRING YOUR OWN APRON.
>
> Sign up at the country store on Wednesday. Old rare comic books, now at "Fun Store."
>
> Beat the Bills! Use wood in your cook stove! www.chopchopwood.chop
>
> BUY A HOME COMFORT THIS WEEK and you'll get a free bark-box made from the very best wood. CALL 000-100-2000 NOW!

Use props, art and music for the presentations.

Activity # 4 (Physical Education, Music, Drama, Dance)
Compose a Waltz for "The Home Comfort"

Use only 3 counts in each measure.

Use props and costumes for the waltz in the presentations.

Activity # 5 (History)
Guest Speaker, Interior Designer

Invite an interior designer to come in and talk about the kitchens of long ago.

Do a Q & A session:
> How much did "The Home Comfort" cost?
>
> Were all wood stoves just like "The Home Comfort"?

Activity #6 (Music)
Guest Speaker, Musician

Invite a fiddler to come into the classroom to play the jig.

Activity #7 (History, English, Drama)
Write a Play or Skit about "The Home Comfort"

Research some facts on:
- Kitchen appliances and cupboard of the 1930's and 40's
- How they heated their homes
- 2 dog nights. (explain to class)

Suggested titles:
- *Readin' My Comics And Feelin' So Warm.*
- *Nobody Knows I'm Back Here*
- *It's Goin' To Be A 3 Dog Night*
- *Too Lazy To Bark*

Be Tricksy and tell how it feels to lay there in the wood box while someone fusses with your puppies.

Activity #8 (Art)
Draw the Scene

Suggestions:
- The Home Comfort Stove
- Tricksy or the puppies getting dressed up
- The girl or boy sitting on the floor in back of the stove reading a comic book
- A loaf of homemade bread with a slice removed
- The wood box

Show and tell about the art at the presentation.

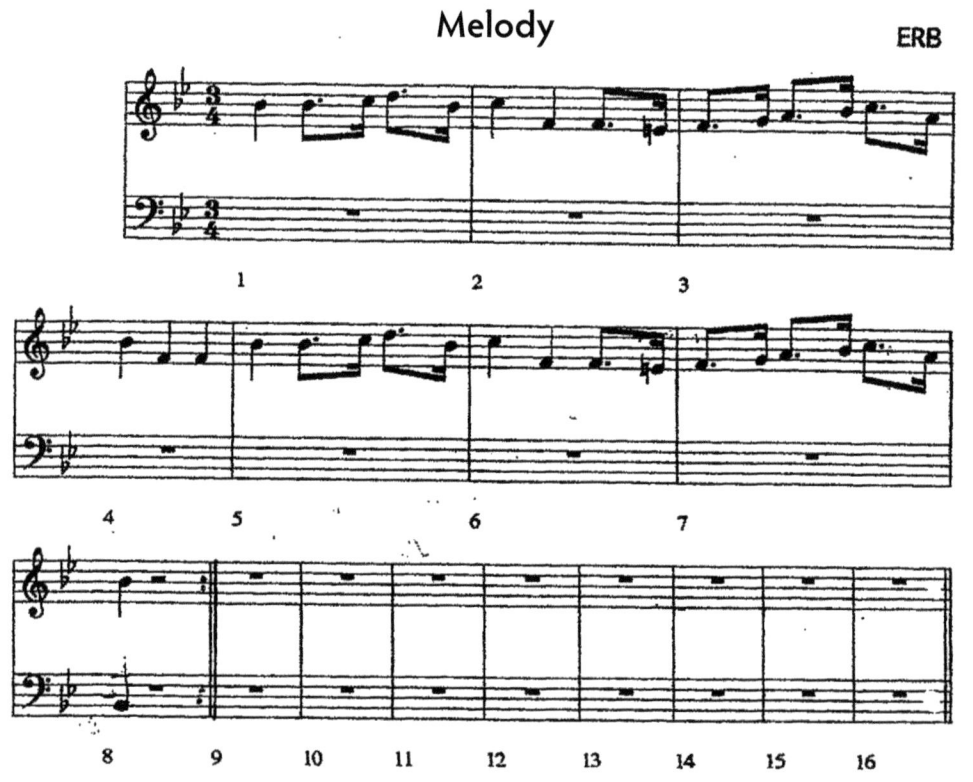

The Home Comfort

WALTZ TEMPO — ELEANOR RUSSELL-BROWN

5

GANDLY

Did you ever wonder how geese know when to take off to begin their flight to the north or south? They say it has something to do with the earth's magnetism, but I wonder.

A goose, named Gandly, landed beside a pond up the road one spring and began to follow a herd of cows. He would eat in the field with them and lay down when they did. He honked when they mooed and huddled with them when they shooed away the flies with their tails.

He thought he was one of the herd.

I will always wonder why Gandly stayed behind when all the other geese flew south or north.

Maybe he decided that because he was a cow he couldn't fly. Or maybe he thought the cows would fly too.

I will never know for sure. Maybe you can think of an answer.

Activity #1 (English, Music)
Compose a Song Gandley

Refer to Aegar's Digger Dance, Activity #4, for instructions on writing a song.

Put a list of vocabulary words on the board: *anser, ninny, solan, raft, yang, cronk, down.*

Have the students look up the words to use in the songs.

Suggestions for song titles:

Goose Down South, Solan, Ninny! Goose Gone Down

I'll Make You Into A Featherbed! Cows and Goose Together.

Sing or play the songs for the presentations.

Activity #2 (English, Drama, Art)
Write a Poem about Gandly

Use the vocabulary words provided in Activity #1.

Suggestions: *Gandley And The Cows. Honk With The Herd. Moo Cronk.*

Students read their poems for the presentations with art and background music.

Activity #3 (Science, English, Drama, Music, Art)
Write and act out a commercial for Gandly

Refer to activity #1 for the vocabulary list for use in the commercial.

Suggestions for titles;

- Magnetic Beaks, by FLOCK, INC.
- "The Flying Cow Restaurant" — cooked goose tonight only, and featuring the group: "THE HONKERS" for your entertainment.
- How to cook a goose in one easy lesson.
- Feather beds, by "BED, BATH AND CRONKERS". For more information call NINNY 11. Cronk out on your feather bed!
- Do some research on the theory of magnetism and how the geese know when to begin their flight south or north.

Use background music and art in the presentations.

Activity #4 (Physical Education, Music, Art, Drama)
Create a dance for Gandly using the jig.

Use costumes and props for the presentations.

Activity #5
Field Trip, Dairy Farm

Take a field trip to a dairy farm for observing the daily operation of milking, feeding, gathering cows from the pasture, etc.

Activity #6 (English, Drama, Music, Art, Science)
Write a play or skit about Gandly.

Use the information found in activity #3 about magnetism to include in the play or skit.
Suggestions:
- Why do geese fly in a V formation?
- What do cows prefer to eat and can a goose eat the same thing?

Learn the vocabulary in activity #1 and use it in the play or skit.
Suggested titles:

Take A Gander! Anser Me! Solan To The Herd!
Who Invited You Here? Gandly's Forced Landing.

Activity #7 (Science)
Guest Speaker, Game Warden/Wild Life Manager

Invite a game warden into the classroom to talk about the laws regarding shooting geese. Have the students write out questions before the session.

Activity #8 (Music)
Guest Musician

Invite a fiddler into the classroom to play the jig plus other tunes in the music section of each story.

6

Saturday Nite

Every Saturday night, over at the Grange Hall, there would be a square dance and a covered dish supper. The Grange Hall was a farmers association.

They had their meetings there and their wives helped out with social events in the farm community. The covered dish suppers were oh, so good - I loved all the casseroles, like scalloped corn and Spanish rice. The homemade rolls were so good that I ate a lot of them with homemade butter slathered all over them.

Then there were all the relishes that had just been put up. I especially liked the piccalilli relish on the rolls.

The pies! Oh, the pies - cherry, blueberry, apple - they were my favorites.

Afterward two fiddlers played waltzes, jigs, and square dances 'til all hours of the night. All the elders sat around the outside against the wall and sometimes you could hear a cane hitting the floor in time to the music.

Activity #1 (Music)
Learn a Round Dance

Teach the round.

If anyone in the class plays an instrument, invite him/her to learn and play the round for the class. Invite a fiddler to come into the class to play the "Saturday Nite Waltz".

Ask her/him to explain the difference between a square, round dance or a waltz.

Invite a square dance group in for a demonstration.

Activity #2 (English, Drama, Music, Art)
Compose a Song about "Saturday Nite"

Follow the directions for writing a song in "Aegar's Digger Dance", activity #4 (page 8)

The song can be made up or can follow the melody for "Saturday Nite".

Suggestions for titles:

Piccalilli Relish. Canes a Tappin'. Grange Hall #29

Perform the songs for presentation.

Activity #3 (English, Drama, Art)
Write and act out a commercial for "Saturday Nite"

Suggestions:
LEARN TO SQUARE DANCE IN 3 EASY LESSONS
NEED A COVERED DISH? CALL "LID inc.
FOR GREAT CANES, CALL "TAP"

Use props and art.

Activity #4 (Physical Education, Music, Dance)
Create a dance to the music for "Saturday Nite"

This activity can involve group dancing, such as round, waltz or square. Or one individual might wish to solo for the presentation.

Use a good piano player to accompany the dances. Use props, costumes and the jig.

Activity #5 (English, Art)
Write a poem about "Saturday Nite"

Suggestions for titles:

Dancing on a Saturday Nite

Squares and Rounds

Illustrate the poem with art. Print out the poems.

Activity #6 (English, Art, Drama)
Write a play or skit about "Saturday Nite"

Research information on the history of the Grange. Include facts in the play or skit.

Suggested titles:
- *Round pies and Square Dances*
- *Saturday Nite Out*
- *Grange Hall #29*

I can't spell Piccalilli, but I can taste it.

Activity #7 (Art)
Draw the scene

Suggestions:
- Fiddles playing
- Feet dancing
- Man with a cane
- Dancers waltzing
- Eating the goodies
- Show and tell for the presentation

Activity #8 (History, Science)
Guest Speakers

Invite a farmer to the class for a lecture about the Grange Hall.

Also invite:
- A bread maker
- A homemaker who knows how to preserve food
- A square dance caller
- A fiddler who can play a waltz or a jig

Have questions ready for a Q&A session.

Suggestions:
- Are there still Grange Halls?
- Why do the farmers belong to it?
- Why does yeast make bread rise?
- How did you learn to play the fiddle — did you take lessons?
- Why does canned food last a long time?

SATURDAY NITE

WALTZ TEMPO

7

Joe Pye

Joe Pye is a weed.

It's a beautiful tall, pink, flowered weed that grew down in our swamp. The Native Americans used the Joe Pye weed as one of their medicines. Joe Pye was a famous Medicine Man, and he used the weed to break a fever.

I guess if you had a bad cold with a temperature back then, Joe Pye would have made you a tea from the weed and you would feel better.

Activity #1 (English, Music)
Compose a Song about "Joe Pye"

Follow the directions for song writing in "Aegar's Digger Dance".

Suggestions for titles: *Pretty Weed, Joe Pye, Tea Time.*

Perform the song for the presentation.

Activity #2 (English, Drama)
Write a Poem about "Joe Pye"

Rhyme words like: *weed, Joe, flower, tea, swamp.*

Try some Haiku.

Suggestions for titles:
- *Tall Pink Flower*
- *Medicine Man*
- *Pull It Out*

Illustrate with art

Each poet can read his/her poem for presentation.

Activity #3 (English, Art, Music)
Draw the scene

Suggestions:
- The Tall Pink Weed.
- Joe Pye, Native American Medicine Man.
- A cup of tea.

Show and tell for the presentation with Indian Drums for background effect.

Activity #4 (English, Art, Drama,)
Write and Act out a Commercial for "Joe Pye"

Suggestions for titles:

CURE YOUR COLD! JOE PYE WEED FOR SALE. CALL JOE TEA-WEED.

JOE PYE, MEDICINE MAN FOR UNUSUAL CURES.

Contact me with smoke signals — third hill over. 3 puffs

Use props, costumes, drums for presentations.

Activity #5 (English, Art, Drama)
Write a play or skit about "Joe Pye"

Suggestions for titles:
- *Don't Pull That Weed!*
- *The Medicine Man Who Cured My Cold*
- *How To Use Native American Medicine*

Use props, art, and costumes.

Activity #6 (Physical Education, Music, Art)
Create a Dance to "Joe Pye"

Use the "Joe Pye" jig for the music. Use props and costumes for the presentations.

Activity #7 (History, Music, Dance)
Guest Speaker

Invite a Native American to the classroom for a talk about their early culture. Ask him or her to perform a Native American dance.

JOE PYE MELODY

ERB

JOE PYE

Allegro
Eleanor Russell-Brown

8

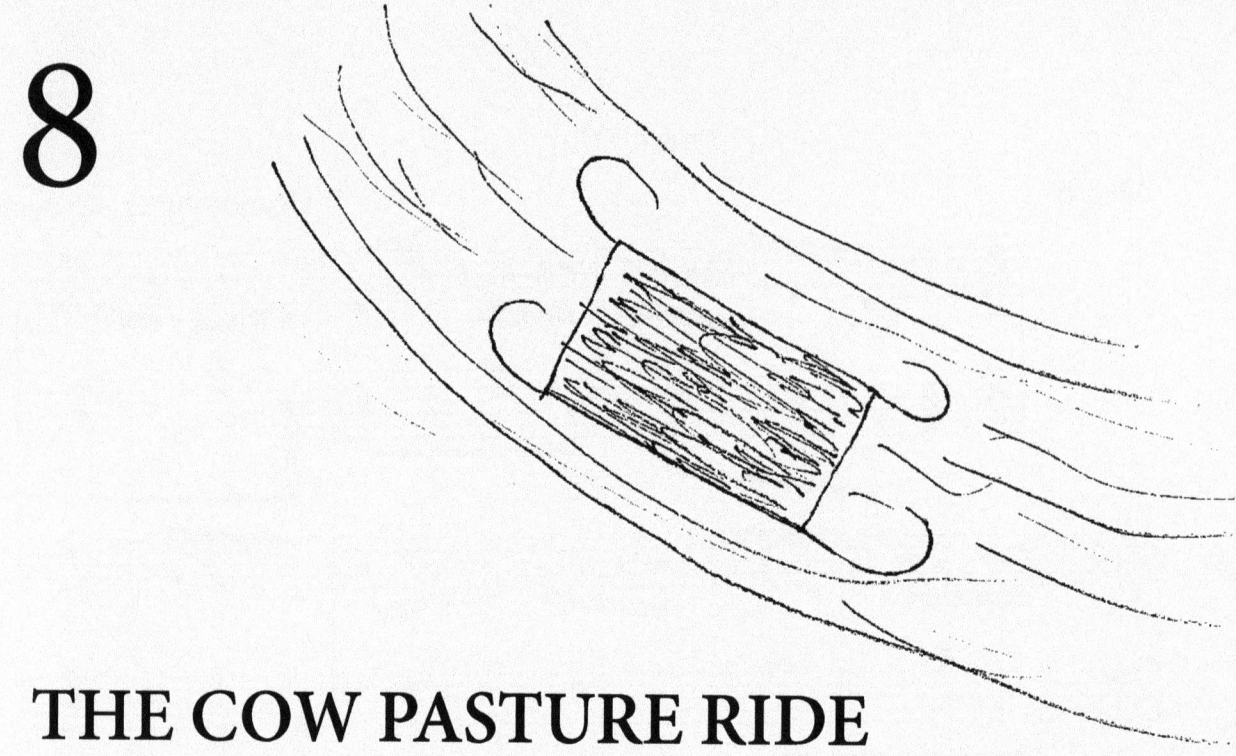

THE COW PASTURE RIDE

Our cow pasture was very hilly and steep in certain places. Cows always find a way to climb a steep hill. They do not climb straight up. They make paths across the hill. So the hill we chose to go sledding on was full of thrills and drop-offs. There were probably four or five paths with great drop-offs that we crossed when sliding down. The biggest drop-off was located near the bottom of the hill.

One Sunday afternoon during a snow storm, we took our sleds to the pasture. Our friend from two farms over came with us. She had a very old, small wooden sled with her. It had two wooden runners on the bottom. There was no steering gear on it.

I went down first and waited at the bottom of the hill while the others slid down. When Mary came to the last drop-off, her sled flew over the huge drop-off and landed with a "Phlump". Both of the runners on the sled gave way and flattened outward when she landed in a cloud of snow.

We rolled in the snow with laughter.

Activity #1 (Music, English)
Compose a Song about The Cow Pasture Ride

Follow the directions in Aegar's Digger Dance, activity #4, for composing a song.

Suggestions for titles:
- *Down Hill Ride. Old Sled*
- *Bumpy Drop-Offs*

Sing or play each song.

Activity #2 (English, Drama, Music, Art)
Write a Poem about The Cow Pasture Ride

Rhyme words like: *hill, path, snow, sled, old, runner.*

Write a Haiku poem. Illustrate with art. Use background music. Read poems to the class, then print them out.

Activity #3 (Art, Music)
Draw the Scene

Suggestions:
- Speeding over the drop-offs on the sled
- The old fashioned sled with only two wooden runners
- The pasture hill
- The girl on the sled as she landed with a "phlump"

Show and tell for the presentations using background music.

Activity #4 (English, Drama, Art)
Write and Act Out a Commercial for The Cow Pasture Ride

Use these vocabulary words in the commercial: *pasture, gear, drop-off, blizzard.*

Activity #5 (English, Art, Drama, Music)
Write a Play or Skit about The Cow Pasture Ride

Suggestions for titles:
- "Phlump"
- Bumps and Thrills Every Time
- What's My Mother Going To Say!
- Sunday Afternoon On The Pasture Hill

Use props, art, music background and costumes for presentations.

Activity #6 (Music, Physical Education)
Create a Dance to The Cow Pasture Ride

Use the jig for the dance music, or invite a fiddler in to play the jig for the dancer.

THE COW PASTURE RIDE

ELEANOR RUSSELL-BROWN

THE COW PASTURE RIDE MELODY

9
CASSIE

A cairn is a heap of stones that was built in Scotland as a monument. The little Scottish dog; the Cairn Terrier, was bred to hunt for rodents in the stones. Our little Cairn Terrier, Cassie, loved to hunt around the farm for mice, rats-anything that was small enough to get rid of. She would sometimes sit for hours waiting for a chipmunk to appear so she could attack.

She was funny too, and she knew that she was funny.

We taught her how to talk. She could say hamburger, mama, out and in. She would have gotten an 'A' in dog English.

Now you had to use your imagination a little when she said "hamburger," but it was there just the same.

When students came to the house for their violin lessons, she rolled over on her back for each one, hoping to get a scratch on her belly, and she was never disappointed.

She had three puppies that were little balls of fur. The kids made a box for her family and they put a sign on the front that read; "CASSIE AND HER CASSETTES."

She begged for people food at the table, and would not eat her dog food until all the lights were turned out at night, then we could hear crunch, crunch out in the kitchen. She was eating her dog food.

She was afraid of thunderstorms and she hid under the bed and would stay there all day sometimes. The only way we could get her to come out was to rattle the cheese wrapper. She would come trotting right out. She loved cheese.

Now she is in dog heaven and is probably teaching other dogs there how to say "hamburger."

Activity #1 (Art)
Make a Cairn Terrier Puppet

Show the class a picture of a Cairn Terrier. Tell about some characteristics of the breed.

Materials:
- sock
- button
- felt-beige or brown colors
- embroidery thread

Activity #2 (Art)
Make a "Pup" Puppet Theater

Materials: see Aegar's Digger Dance, activity #2 on page 6

Activity #3 (Drama, Music)
Put on a "Pup" Puppet Show

Use the jig for background music to tell the story of Cassie and her "Cassettes."

Activity #4 (Music, English)
Compose a Song about Cassie

Follow the directions in Aegar's Digger Dance.

Suggestions for titles:
- *Hamburger, Mama, In, Out*
- *I Can't Believe It's a Talking Dog!*
- *Dog Gone It!*
- *Thunder And The Cheese*

Perform the songs at the presentations.

Activity #5 (English)
Write a Poem about Cassie

Rhyme words like: *cairn, dog, puppy, terrier, scot, talk, mama*

Activity #6 (Art, Music)
Draw the Scene

Suggestions:
- A Cairn Terrier
- Cassie in the box with her cassettes
- Cassie eating her food after dark
- Cassie at the door saying "out"
- Cassie begging at the table saying "hamburger"

Show and tell with music background for the presentations.

Activity #7 (Drama, Music, English, Art)
Write and Act out a Commercial About Cassie

Suggestions:

CASSIE'S SCHOOL OF DOG LANGUAGE---CALL 555-ad.

TEACH YOUR DOG TO TALK IN 2 EASY LESSONS!

www.mamahamburger.corn DOG GONE IT!

Use props costumes, art, and music. Film the presentations.

Activity #8 (Drama, Music, English, Art)
Write a Play or Skit About Cassie

Look up some facts about Scotland to be included in the play or skit.

Suggestions for research:
- Why is the Cairn Terrier a Scottish dog?
- Why are the Cairn Terrier's legs so short?
- Where is Scotland?
- Is their language English?

Suggestions for titles:
- *Say "cheese".*
- *You say there's cheese in my dog food?*
- *My Scottish bark.*

Other suggestions:
- I'm in doggie heaven teaching other dogs to talk.
- Be a Cairn Terrier and express how it feels to say people words.

Use props, art, music background (jigs) for presentations.

Film the productions.

10

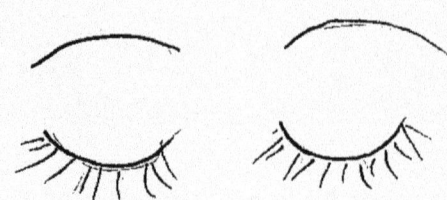

Dreams That I Dreamed

A deep rill flowed through the pine trees down in our woods. When I went to gather the cows in the pasture to bring them back to the barn for milking, I dawdled by the little tiny deep creek.

I would find stones and sticks and play in the water. I daydreamed about what I would be someday.

Sometimes I wanted to be a famous pianist. Other times I dreamed of being rich so I might live in a great big house with pillars on the front and my bedroom would look out on a huge green lawn. What if I were a doctor? I could make little kids well.

But I never became any of those things, nor did I have a house with pillars. I did have a piano though, and I can play it, but I'm not famous.

Activity #1 (Music)
Compose a Song for "Dreams That I Dreamed"

Follow the directions in "Aegar's Digger Dance"

Suggestions for titles:
- *What Would I Like to Be?*
- *I'm Just A Daydreamer*
- *Maybe I'll Be Famous*

Activity #2 (English, Art)
Write a poem about "Dreams That I Dreamed"

Rhyme words like: *woods, rill, creek, stones, piano, nurse, house, dream.*

Try some Haiku poetry.

Suggestions for titles:
- *Dreamer*
- *Down By The Rill*
- *My House*

Illustrate with art for the presentation.

Activity #3 (Art, Music)
Draw the scene

Suggestions:
- Dreamy eyes
- Scene with the rill running through the woods
- Big house with the pillars

Show and tell for the presentation with music background.

Activity # 4 (English, Drama, Music)
Write and Act out a Commercial "Dreams That I Dreamed"

Put these vocabulary words on the board to learn and use in the commercial:

rill, pillars, piano, pine trees

Suggestions:

Dream Your Way to Riches! Yes, You can be rich just by dreaming! LOG ON TO $.com.

You will see the secrets of getting rich! Buy that house you've always dreamed of!

Call "A BIG HOUSE". We'll make your dreams come true!

WANT TO BE FAMOUS? Play the piano in just 10 easy lessons! Make big money play for people and events. Piano Lessons Right on the Internet! fame. corn

Activity #5
Write a Play or Skit about "Dreams That I Dreamed"

Suggestions for titles:
- *Could you please bring the cows home?*
- *Where the deep rill flows*

Use props, costumes and background music for presentations.

Activity #6 (Psychology)
Guest Speaker

Invite a psychologist to the classroom to talk about what dreams mean. Ask what daydreaming means and why we do it.

Activity #7 (Music)
Guest Musician

Invite a piano major from a college or an advanced piano student to come and play for the class. Have a Q&A session.

Activity #8 (Physical Education, Music, Drama, Art)
Create a Dance to "Dreams That I Dreamed"

Use the "Dreams" music for the dance.

Use props and costumes — especially silky scarves.

DREAMS THAT I DREAMED MELODY

DREAMS THAT I DREAMED

WALTZ TEMPO

ELEANOR RUSSELL-BROWN

11
The DD Tree

The "DD Tree" was huge. It had roots that went all the way down a steep bank. There was a hole at the bottom where the immense roots twisted around each other.

My sister and I discovered the hole one day while we were exploring down on the bank. We stepped between the knotted roots and when we got to the hole, all sorts of secret places behind the roots were revealed to us.

We decided to call this place the "DD Tree." The DD would be our secret code - the two Ds' being in the word "hidden."

Upon returning to the house, we searched for containers to put treasures in. We found some old cigar boxes in the cellar - perfect, we thought.

We began to dig for our treasures in the old dump in back of the house. We found pieces of interesting green glass, an old button, part of a little glass doll, a piece of a small chain, and a marble, which my sister tried to get away from me. We finally traded her red bead, that she later found, for my marble.

Now our boxes were full of "DDs." We took our treasure boxes to the "DD Tree" and hid them. We visited the tree all summer with new items to put in with other findings. We talked and pretended about the treasures.

Who owned the bead? Were the pieces of glass, dishes? Who played with the marble and would there be more where we found that one?

We continued to dig in the old dump all the rest of summer, but we never did find more marbles.

The treasures in the cigar boxes sat on a shelf in our bedroom for a long time after that. Sometimes I would take them all out and spread them on my bed, then I put them back in the box.

The "DD Tree" is still there, bigger than ever, but I don't think either myself or my sister could fit in the hole behind those roots any more.

Activity #1
Make a Treasure Box

Materials:

- cardboard
- paste or glue
- markers, paints or crayons
- all kinds of buttons, beads, ribbon, wallpaper, newspaper, cutouts of animals or flowers, bling
- scissors
- construction paper
- paint brush
- colored tissue paper

Activity #2
Have a Treasure Trade

1. Each student brings a wrapped treasure to school.
2. The treasures are placed in a box.
3. The students line up and remove a treasure out of the box without looking at it.
4. A student is chosen to come forward with his/her treasure. He/ she asks if there is
5. anyone who wants to trade for his/her found object.
6. The trade takes place.
7. The trading keeps taking place until the last person in the class has traded.
8. Now everyone has a new treasure for their box and can open it.

Activity #3
Compose a song about the DD TREE

Follow the directions in Aegar's Digger Dance, activity #4, for writing a song.

Suggestions for titles:

- The Old Dump
- My House is Old
- They Threw The Junk In The Dump
- Treasures Down In The Tree

Perform the songs for the presentations.

Activity #4 (Science)
Research Types of Trees in Your Area

- Find a tree that might have huge roots that spread
- Find a tree that looses it's leaves in the winter
- What kind of bird might build its' nest in the "DD TREE"
- Could a house be built out of the kind of wood in any of the trees?
- How do you tell how old a tree is?
- What color are the fall leaves from some of the trees?

Show and tell in the presentations.

Activity #5 (English, Art, Music)
Write a poem about "THE DD TREE"

Use some words for rhyming like: dump, bead, tree, roots, treasure, box, trade, marble.

Write some Haiku. Illustrate with art.

Read the poems for the presentations with music background.

Activity #6 (Physical Education, Dance, Drama, Music, Art)
Create a Dance for "THE DD TREE"

Use the jig for the dance.

Use props and costumes in the presentations.

Activity #7 (English, Drama, Music, Art)
Write a play or skit about "THE DD TREE"

Use some of the research facts found in Activity 4 for the production.

Suggestions for titles:
- *Dig It And Hide It*
- *Unknown Treasures*
- *Do You Dig It?*

Use props, art, costumes, and music for presentations.

Activity #8 (English, Drama, Music, Art)
Write and Act Out a Commercial for THE DD TREE

Suggestions for titles:

HAVE YOU LOST YOUR MARBLES? www.gettotherootoftheproblem.tree

Treasure Hunt on Saturday, June 5th over at Digger Dells. The great archeologist, Dr. Digging, will show you what to look for and how to dig for great treasures.

Use props, costumes, art, and music for the presentations.

Activity #9 (English)
Write a Story about Treasure

Write a story about your own found treasures and the ones that you will keep forever. Tell why you will always want them.

Activity #10
View a Movie

Watch a movie of *Treasure Island*.

Activity #11
Field Trip to Museum

Go on a field trip to a museum for viewing artifacts from around the world.

Activity #12 (Science, Archeology)
Guest Speaker, Archeologist

Invite an archeologist to come and talk about digs in countries like Egypt and artifacts found right here in the U.S.

Have a Q & A session following his talk.

Activity #13 (Science, Enviromental Studies)
Guest Speaker, Environmentalist

Invite an environmentalist or forester to speak about the trees in the rain forest and why they are so vital to the balance of life on earth.

THE DD TREE

ERB

12

THE SUGAR SLED

Every spring, usually in March, the sap begins to flow out of the maple trees. We had a lot of those kind of trees down in our woods. I loved riding on the sled with my father to gather the sap from the trees.

First he had to tap the tree and put in a spigot. After that he hung a metal bucket on the spigot. Then after a few days, we would ride down again on the sled with the empty buckets clanging against each other. We gathered the sap and brought it back to the open barn.

My father built a huge log fire underneath the vats where the sap boiled. By the end of the day, the sap was thick and sugary. The air around the farm smelled so good!

We bottled the thick, sweet syrup and sold it out in front of the house in a little stand that we used for selling vegetables and fruit later on in the summer.

Sometimes my stepmother boiled the sap down on our Home Comfort wood stove and when the sap became syrup, we poured the stringy syrup over a tub of snow. It was called Sugar Candy. A tasty Treat!

Activity #1 (Music, English)
Compose a Song about "The Sugar Sled"

Follow the directions for writing a song in "Aegar's Digger Dance"

The melody provided with the story can also be used. Just add words.

Suggestions for titles:
- *Who Ever Heard Of Sugar From A Tree!*
- *My Sweet Tooth*
- *The Candy Tree*
- *A Sled Full Of Sweets*
- *I Love To Sip The Sap*

Sing or play the songs for the presentations.

Activity #2 (English, Music, Drama)
Write a Poem about "The Sugar Sled"

Explain and use these vocabulary words: *sap, maple, vat, tree, spigot.*

Use the words in the poem for rhyming.

Each student who selected this activity read his/her poem to the class.

Print out the poems for the students.

Activity #3 (English, Art, Music, Drama)
Write and Act out a Commercial for "The Sugar Sled"

Suggestions:

Sweet treat at Sam's Syrup Shed — Just follow your nose to the road that leads into the woods. The Maple trees await you.

For good maple syrup, phone BUCKET BRIGADE FARM.

For all your sugaring-off equipment go to: SNOWJOB.YUM

Use props, art and jig melody.

Activity #4 (Physical Education, Dance, Music)
Create a Dance for "The Sugar Sled"

Use the jig melody. Use props and costumes.

Activity #5 (Science)
Visit a tree farm

Visit a tree farm to learn about the different kinds of trees in your area.

Write down your questions before you go.

Activity #6 (English, Art, Music, Drama)
Write a Play or Skit about "The Sugar Sled"

Suggestions for titles:

My Sweet tooth.

The Horse Who Loved To Sip the Sap

When March Comes

The Sap Runs.

Use props, costumes, art and music for presentations.

Activity #7 (Science, History)
Guest Speaker, Tree Farmer

Invite a farmer into the classroom who makes and sells maple syrup.

Have some questions ready:

- What makes the sap flow from the trees?
- Do maple trees shed their leaves in the fall?
- Does the sap have a taste?
- Why can't you make syrup out of other trees?
- What is sugar snow?

Activity #8 (Music)
Guest Musician

Invite a fiddler into the classroom to play the jig.

Activity #9 (Art, English)
Draw the scene

Suggestions:

- A sugar sled
- A maple tree with a sap bucket hanging from it
- A maple syrup stand out in front of the old farmhouse
- A boy or girl feeding one of the horses a maple sugar cube
- The shed where the sap is boiled down

Show and tell about the drawing.

THE SUGAR SLED MELODY

ERB

SUGAR SLED

Sugar Sled p.2

13

KITTENS IN THE HAYSTACK

There were fourteen cats on our farm. They were always in the barn at milking time and my father would squirt milk at one or another of them who happened to be sitting nearby.

I noticed one cat who seemed to get fatter and fatter by the day. She was going to have kittens! Soon! I wanted to be sure to follow her to find out where she would go to have them. I knew she would try to hide them.

Every morning I would fly out of bed early, get dressed for school, gobble down my breakfast, and head for the barn. I followed her, but she would just stop and wash her paws. She took so long, as if to tease me. I had to get the bus and I couldn't wait for her to reveal her hiding place.

I continued to watch her every night at milking time. She grew bigger all the time until she looked like she would burst. Then one night she appeared much thinner when she came to wait for her squirt of milk. I knew she had had her kittens! But where?

The next day I did my morning things and then ran to the barn. I gave my brother orders as to where to search. I would look somewhere else. We hunted everywhere; even in the root cellar, the last place where a cat would have her kittens.

Then I went to one corner of the hay mound upstairs and that's when I heard little tiny mews coming from way down in the hay beside a beam. What we found were six beautiful, long haired, calico kittens. We picked each one up and looked it over.

Everyone wanted one of them, so when they got weaned from their mother, they went to new homes around the neighborhood.

I bet that those farmers didn't have any more trouble with pesky little mice.

Activity #1 (Music, English, Drama)
Compose a Song about "Kittens In The Haystack"

Follow the directions in "Aegar's Digger Dance", activity #4, for writing the song.

Suggestions for titles:

> *Fourteen Cats Lookin' for Milk*
>
> *Fat Cat Calicos*

The students will sing or play their songs for presentations.

Activity #2 (English, Drama)
Create a poem about "Kittens In The Haystack"

Rhyme words like: *kitten, milk, hay, fat, barn, mice.* Write some Haiku.

Suggestioned titles:

> *Long-haired Calico*
>
> *Meows for a Drink*
>
> *Bigger and Bigger*
>
> *Tiny Meows*

Students read poems. Print out poems.

Activity #3 (Art, English, Music)
Draw the Scene

Suggestions:
- Little kittens way down by a beam in the hay.
- The fat mother cat sitting in back of the cows waiting for a squirt of milk.
- A barn with lots of cats wandering around.
- A cat chasing a mouse.

Show the presentation using background music.

Activity #4 (Drama, Art, English, Music)
Write and Act in a Commercial for "Kittens In The Haystack"

Use these vocabulary words in the commercial: *root cellar, calico, haystack, wean*

Suggestions for titles:

> Long haired calico kittens are available now!
> HURRY! GOING FAST! CALL "ME-OUSER".
> Train your cat at "FELINE OBEDIENCE SCHOOL".
> Log on to catfight.
> Meow for expert cat handling! GOT MICE? We have the answer to your problem!
> CALL "RENT-A-MEOW".

Use props, art, and costumes for presentations.

Activity #5 (English, Drama, Art, Music)
Write a play about "Kittens In The Haystack"

Suggestions for titles:
- *The Day I Missed The bus*
- *The Great Cat Hunt*

Show and act out presentation with background music.

Activity #6 (Science)
Guest Speaker, Veterinarian

Invite a veterinarian to the classroom to talk about cats. Have questions ready.
- Why are cats born with their eyes closed?
- Why do some cats have seven toes?

KITTENS IN THE HAYSTACK MELODY — ERB

KITTENS IN THE HAYSTACK

ELEANOR RUSSELL-BROWN

14

Fiddle In The Attic

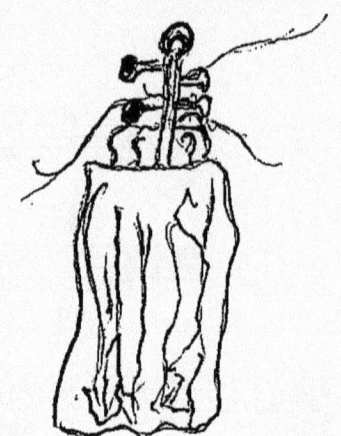

Our attic, like most attics, was crammed full of things we didn't want. Old toys, boxes of whatever, clothes—just about anything you could think of.

My sister and I often dressed up in the old clothes from the trunk.

One day as I bent over to explore, I spied a string sticking out of some junk. I pulled on it and heard a sound, like a "boing." I moved some stuff away from the string and as I uncovered layers of papers, the top part of a fiddle appeared. It stuck out from the top of a paper sack.

I lifted it out and found that all the strings were broken, two pegs were missing, and whatever else the strings were supposed to be attached to was missing.

I carried the fiddle downstairs and asked my stepmother how it got in the attic. She didn't know and knew nothing about fiddles.

We ran to the barn with the fiddle under my arm and asked my father about it. He replied that a man had brought the fiddle to him one day as a trade for some chickens. He just put the fiddle in the attic and never thought about it after that.

We took it to a repair person who put it in playing condition. When he called to let us know that the work had been completed, we asked if he knew anything about the fiddle.

"Well," he answered, "What you have here is a six-thousand dollar violin. It is signed by the maker." He showed us the signature inside of the violin.

Were we flabbergasted? Yeah! And I got to take lessons on it!

Activity #1 (Music, English)
Compose a song about "Fiddle In The Attic"

Follow the directions in "Aegar's Digger Dance", activity #4, for writing a song.
Provide the following list of vocabulary words for learning the parts of a violin:

bridge, scroll, bow, resin, horsehair, body, finger board.

Suggestions for titles:

The Bow Hair, Found Fiddle, Fiddling Around, No Strings Attached
Perform the song.

Activity #2 (English)
Write a poem about "The Fiddle In The Attic"

Rhyme words like: *fiddle, bow, string, peg, play, notes, music*
Suggestions for titles:

- *Stringing Along*
- *The Attic*
- *Draw The Bow*
- *Make The Fiddle Mine*

Activity #3 (Art)
Draw the scene

Suggestions for titles:
- The broken string sticking up out of the sack
- A student taking lessons on the violin
- A shocked face when told the value of the violin
- A fiddle with no strings attached

Show and tell for the presentation with background music

Activity #4 (English, Drama, Art, Music)
Write and act out a commercial for "Fiddle In The Attic"

Suggestions:
Free fiddle Lessons — NO STRINGS ATTACHED!
LOG ON TO dontknowhowtoplay.boing or call 1234HITIT!
RARE ATTIC FINDS, by JUNK & STUFF.
Will go through your attic, clean it out, and tell you what you've got!
For good Bow Hair, call WHINNIE. We offer the best horsetails.
Use props, art, costumes for presentations.

Activity #5 (Physical Education, Music, Dance, Art)
Create a dance to "Fiddle In The Attic"

Use props, costumes and the jig (next page) for presentations.

Activity #6 (English, Music, Art, Drama)
Write a play or skit about "The Fiddle In The Attic"

Suggestions for titles:
- *This Fiddle Isn't Worth A Nickle! Teach Me How To Play!*
- *What Was That "Boing" Sound? My Horse Has Bow Hair*

Use props and costumes for the presentations.

Activity #7 (Music)
Guest Musician

Invite a violin teacher to come in for a talk about violin lessons. Have questions ready.
- What makes a violin valuable?
- Why do you make the bow hair out of a horse's tail?
- What does the resin do?
- Will you play a jig for us?

Activity #8 (Music, History)
Field Trip to Symphony or Concert

Plan a field trip to a symphony rehearsal or concert.

Beforehand, talk about what to look for and listen for in the orchestra and music

Talk about concert manners.

15

PHOEBE

My father gave me baby animals when I was about ten or eleven. I loved the little piglet he presented to me one day. I named her Phoebe.

I carried her around and dressed her in old clothes. She became so attached to me she followed me everywhere, even down through the pasture when I went to get the cows for milking.

She didn't like it when I went into the house and left her outside by herself. I told my father she "oink-wailed."

She grew and grew until she finally weighed four hundred pounds. She got so big she could not follow me any more. I went out to her pen and sat with her while I ate my apples and she ate her slop.

Then one day my father came in from the barn and announced that Phoebe had given birth to five piglets.

I ran out to her pen immediately, opened the fence and went in. I approached Phoebe and petted her. Then I picked up one of the piglets. I was cuddling it when I heard a loud squeal. I looked up. Phoebe had gotten up and she was going to charge me. The other piglets were still hanging on to her as she ran.

I don't remember putting the piglet down, but in my haste to run, I must have. She chased me right out of her pen.

I decided I wouldn't want to have another pig for a pet—they just don't stay friends forever.

Activity #1 (Music, English)
Compose a Song about Phoebe

Follow the directions in "Aegar's Digger Dance" for composing a song.

The melody can be made up by the student, or the student can use the melody provided for "PHOEBE." Write words to the song.

Suggestions for titles:
- Five Little Piglets
- Phoebe Doesn't Like Me Anymore
- Friends Forever, Maybe

The song can be sung by the teacher or by the student composer.

Activity #2 (English, Art, Drama)
Write a Poem about Phoebe

Suggestions for words for rhyming: *pig, hog, fat, piggy, pen, friend, pal*

Suggestions for titles:
- *No Pal of Mine*
- *What's Your Problem, Phoebe?*
- *Pens and Pigs*

Illustrate the poem with art. Poetry reading by students.

Print out all the poems for the students to keep.

Activity #3 (English, Art, Drama, Music)
Write and Act Out a Commercial for Phoebe

Use props, costumes, music and art for the presentations.

Suggestions:

PIG-PALS AROUND THE WORLD.

Contact one anywhere by logging on to: oinkoink

The newest book in the Phoebe Series is now on the bookshelves for only $24.95.

Better Hurry! They're going fast!

FIND OUT WHAT HAPPENS AFTER ONE PIGLET COMES UP MISSING!

NEED TO LOSE WEIGHT? CALL PORK ANONYMOUS! 400-300-200

GOING GOING GONE!

Activity #4 (Art, English)
Draw the Scene

Suggestions:
- Phoebe
- The Piglets
- Phoebe Chasing The Girl
- Phoebe "oink-wailing" because she can't come into the house

Show and tell about the scene using the jig as background music.

Activity #5 (Physical Education, Music, Dance)
Create a Dance to the Phoebe music

Use props and costumes for presentations.

Activity #6 (English, Drama, Art)
Write a Play or Skit about Phoebe

Suggestions for titles:
- Mad Pigs!
- Help! Pig Attack!
- What Cute Little Piglets!

Use props and costumes.

Be Phoebe and express how you feel when your piglet gets picked up.

Activity #7 (Social Studies, Science)
Guest Speaker, Farmer

Invite a farmer to come to the classroom to talk about pigs.

Activity #8 (Music)
Guest Musician

Invite a fiddler to come in to the classroom to play the jig.

Activity #9 (Social Studies, Science)
Field Trip

Take a field trip to a farm that has different kinds of pigs.

PHOEBE

ELLY BROWN

www.ingramcontent.com/pod-product-compliance
Ingram Content Group UK Ltd.
Pitfield, Milton Keynes, MK11 3LW, UK
UKHW050414240426
12048UKWH00020B/1514